JUST BE YOU

T0343542

JUST BE YOU

An Hachette UK Company
www.hachette.co.uk

Vie Books, an imprint of Summersdale Publishers Ltd
Part of Octopus Publishing Group Limited
Carmelite House
50 Victoria Embankment
LONDON
EC4Y 0DZ
UK

www.summersdale.com

Printed and bound in Poland

ISBN: 978-1-80007-342-5

Substantial discounts on bulk quantities of Summersdale books are available to corporations, professional associations and other organizations. For details contact general enquiries: telephone: +44 (0) 1243 771107 or email: enquiries@summersdale.com.

Neither the author nor the publisher can be held responsible for any loss or claim arising out of the use, or misuse, of the suggestions made herein. None of the views or suggestions in this book are intended to replace medical opinion from a doctor. If you have any concerns about your health, please seek professional advice.

JUST BE YOU

Embrace Your Greatness
and Be Brilliantly You

POPPY O'NEILL

CONTENTS

FOREWORD

In today's world there seems to be an ever-increasing number of obstacles that teenagers and young people are expected to navigate and overcome. These obstacles permeate every aspect of a young person's life – at home, at school, with friends and online – and cover a wide range of issues, including bullying, social comparisons, having to meet unrealistic expectations and poor self-image. This is all at a time when they are undergoing significant physical, emotional and hormonal changes. As a result of all of these challenges, it is little wonder that teenagers seem to be facing an epidemic of low self-worth.

This new book from Poppy O'Neill explores this critical issue of self-worth in a highly accessible and readable way and will act as a significant resource to help teenagers and their families understand and work with these issues, especially at a time when mental health resources in this country are so overstretched.

The book starts with an introduction to self-worth, what it is, what impacts it, what high levels of self-worth feel like and what low levels feel like. From there, Poppy explores a variety of ways of boosting self-worth, overcoming self-doubt and taking good care of yourself. Each of the strategies presented have been shown to be clinically effective and include CBT (cognitive behavioural therapy) and mindfulness.

I highly recommend this book and hope that it goes at least some way to help teenagers to not only recognize what is causing their self-worth issues but to build a toolbox of strategies to help them address both the symptoms and the underlying issues.

Graham Kennedy MA, UKCP Reg
Integrative Child & Adolescent Psychotherapist
Attachment and Trauma Consultant

January 2022

INTRODUCTION

Welcome to *Just Be You*, a book about being yourself and growing your self-worth. When you know who you are and have a healthy sense of self-worth, you can move through life with confidence and feel secure in yourself and your capabilities.

Being yourself sounds simple, but it can get tricky during your teenage years. Your brain is developing at an incredible rate – meaning you're full of creativity and potential. It also means you're more vulnerable to pressure and negative messages from others and the world around you. Friends, influencers, teachers, parents and the media all bombarding you with different messages about how you should look, think and feel... sometimes you just have to wonder: can I just be me?

The good news is, yes you can! The bad news is, it's hard sometimes. There's a lot of pressure on you to fit in, and being true to yourself takes a lot of guts. In this book you'll find ideas, tools and strategies used by therapists to help you shift how you think about yourself and find your place in the world.

IT'S OK NOT TO FEEL OK

Sometimes it feels like everyone else has it all figured out. Other people seem to go around being themselves, fitting in and living their best lives, while you're left wondering where to begin.

The truth is, no one has it all figured out... especially while they're a teenager. This is the time you get to work out who you are, what you like and what you believe in. Sounds great when you put it like that, but in reality it can feel confusing, difficult and even downright terrifying.

It's OK if you're struggling, and it's OK to need help. It's OK if there are parts of your childhood life that you want to hold onto, or miss, or feel embarrassed about, and it's also OK if you want to hit fast forward and get to adulthood asap. It's OK to change your mind, try things out and say "no". So, take a deep breath and remember that being yourself – exactly as you are right now – is all you need to do.

Basically, whatever you're going through, you never need to deal with it alone, and it's all part of the difficult, messy, creative process of being alive.

WHAT THIS BOOK WILL DO FOR YOU

This book will help you understand how self-worth works, and why being yourself and staying true to yourself is sometimes really hard. It'll also show you how to stand up for yourself, build up your self-worth and keep it high, even when things get tough.

The more you learn about yourself and how your mind works, the more in control of your thoughts, feelings and actions you'll be.

If you're sick of keeping quiet and going along with the crowd just to fit in, and you're ready to change how you think and feel about yourself, this book is for you. Using a mix of ideas and activities, *Just Be You* will guide you through practical ways of shifting your point of view, so you can feel more positive about who you are.

You're already a strong, brilliant person with loads to offer the world, and this book will help you be unapologetically you. So read on and remember: you're awesome exactly as you are.

Self-worth
Noun

How much value you place on yourself, and how much respect you believe you deserve.

HOW TO USE THIS BOOK

This book is for you if...

★ **You hide things about yourself in order to fit in**

★ **You feel like you should look or act more like other people, and less like you**

★ **You feel jealous often**

★ **You compare yourself to others**

★ **You keep quiet when you disagree with someone**

★ **You say "yes" when you really want to say "no" (and vice versa)**

★ **You feel like there's something wrong or weird about you as a person**

★ **You worry about what other people think of you**

If this sounds like you sometimes, or maybe all the time, this book is here to help. Being yourself can be tough, but you have the power to change how you think and feel about yourself for the better.

Inside, you'll find information and ideas that will help you build up your self-worth, so you can feel more comfortable and confident in yourself.

This book is about you, so remember that you're the expert and there are no wrong answers. It's about being curious and interested in your mind, rather than working out if there's something wrong with you. It's also OK to go at your own pace – some of the things in the book will feel useful and others not so much. You are the boss and it's fine to go with what feels right for you.

PART 1:

SELF-WORTH AND YOU

WHAT'S IT LIKE BEING YOU?

Everyone is different, and you are one of a kind. How you feel about yourself has a big effect on your life, and getting to know yourself is the first step toward positive self-worth. In this chapter we'll explore what it's like to be you, as well as how young people feel about self-worth.

ALL ABOUT ME

Learning about yourself and what's important to you is a really important part of growing a healthy sense of self-worth. The better you know yourself, the easier it is to be yourself and stand your ground in any situation. Here are some prompts to get you thinking. Write your answers in the spaces, or grab a notebook if you want to write more!

My name is...

My family is...

Something that always cheers me up is...

If I had to eat the same meal every day for the rest of my life, I'd eat...

My favourite book is...

At the moment I'm learning...

I feel embarrassed when...

Something that freaks me out is...

Three ways I've changed since
I was a young kid...

My earliest memory is...

It's so annoying when...

If I were an animal, I'd be...

WHAT IS SELF-WORTH?

Self-worth

noun

Respect for one's own character and abilities; the feeling of being comfortable with oneself.

Self-worth is all about how much respect you show yourself. When you have high self-worth, you're in tune with your feelings and you stand up for yourself, even when it's unpopular or difficult. If you have low self-worth, you put other people's feelings before your own, ignoring or keeping quiet about your own needs and opinions.

Most people are somewhere in between, and our sense of self-worth can go up or down depending on our experiences, influences and the environment around us. As everyone is unique, the way your self-worth works will be unique too. At its root, self-worth is about how comfortable you feel being yourself, and how much you are able to accept and show kindness to your thoughts, feelings and actions.

But self-worth is also about other people. When you have high self-worth, you can accept yourself *and* others for who they are, even when you're very different from each other. That's because feeling comfortable with yourself means knowing you don't need to be like everybody else – and that not everybody needs to like you – so it feels easy to show respect in any situation.

WHAT IS MENTAL HEALTH?

Everybody has mental health. Just like physical health, it can go up and down, and when it gets bad we need rest and help from others. One of the big differences between mental and physical health is that, while our bodies are all different, they all work in a similar way. Yet when it comes to mental health, everybody's mind works in a unique way.

But physical and mental health are closely linked. When you take good care of your body, you take good care of your mind too. Things like eating healthily, drinking plenty of water and getting enough sleep will help your brain function well – because it's a part of your body. In the same way, emotional self-care like taking breaks and standing up for yourself are good for your physical health because they reduce stress and anxiety.

DO NOT ALLOW PEOPLE TO DIM YOUR SHINE BECAUSE THEY ARE BLINDED. TELL THEM TO PUT ON SOME SUNGLASSES.

Lady Gaga

WHAT HIGH SELF-WORTH FEELS LIKE

Feeling hopeful for the future	Feeling comfortable in your own company	Saying "no" to things you don't want	Knowing you're a good person
Feeling OK to disagree	Encouraging others	Respecting differences	Having your own interests
Feeling OK with making mistakes	Wearing clothes you feel comfortable in	Speaking up when you're unhappy	Taking good care of your body
Feeling comfortable changing your mind	Saying "yes" to opportunities you're excited about	Speaking your mind	Celebrating your achievements

WHAT LOW SELF-WORTH FEELS LIKE

Feeling down about yourself	Thinking you need to be perfect	Feeling jealous	Putting others down
Doing things just to fit in	Spending time with people who are unkind to you	Keeping quiet to avoid disagreements	Needing to make other people agree with you
Never feeling good enough	Saying "yes" when you want to say "no"	Thinking you don't deserve good things	Trying to avoid or deny your emotions
Needing likes and compliments to feel good	Not looking after your body	Spending too much time on social media	Going along with the crowd

HOW SELF-WORTH AFFECTS YOUR LIFE

Low self-worth can impact your life in all sorts of ways. Here are just a few examples.

> The group of friends I hang out with are really horrible to each other. Every week one of us gets picked on by the others because of something small.

> I dress like the other girls in my year so I don't stick out. I think the more individual kids actually look pretty cool, but I'm not brave enough to dress how I want.

> I had the opportunity to go abroad with my rugby team, but I said "no" because I was worried about losing the game.

When I feel anxious, I scroll social media for hours. I don't feel able to talk about my anxiety with anyone.

My friends and I go to the cinema a lot, but we never seem to see the films I want to watch. I wish I had the guts to stand up for myself, but what if they don't like the film I choose?

THE SELF-WORTH QUIZ

Take this quiz to get to know your self-worth levels a little better. Circle the answer that sounds most like you... results are on the next page.

I'm unique because...

a)   I have my own strengths, weaknesses and personality

b)   I'm better than most of the people I know

c)   Everyone else finds it easy to fit in

How easygoing are you?

a)   I'm pretty easygoing, but I can stand up for myself when it matters

b)   I like to get my own way most of the time

c)   I'm very easygoing; I'll go along with what other people want

When there's a conflict or disagreement, I...

a)   Stay calm and think about my response

b)   Get angry and raise my voice

c)   Stay quiet and often just end up pretending to agree

When I think about my future...

a)   I'm excited but nervous too – I have big plans!

b)   I know exactly how it'll go

c)   I feel scared or sad

My friends are...

    a)   My biggest cheerleaders; we support each other no matter what

    b)   Always looking for ways to put each other down

    c)   OK, I guess

When I'm having a hard time, I...

    a)   Talk about my feelings with someone I trust

    b)   Ignore my feelings until they go away

    c)   Keep my feelings to myself

Mostly As: you have a really healthy sense of self-worth. You respect yourself enough to speak up when it matters, and you have bags of respect for others too. You've got a good group of friends, and you know who you are. This book will help you find out lots more about yourself, as well as recognize the signs of low self-worth.

Mostly Bs: you have low self-worth, but you try and hide it. You struggle with not feeling good enough, so you put on a front to appear confident. Building up your self-worth and self-respect isn't easy, but you've got the strength to do it.

Mostly Cs: you have low self-worth, and it's really getting you down. The way you think and feel about yourself can change, and you have the ability to change it for the better. Strengthening your self-worth will improve your life in so many ways, and you have everything you need to start making positive changes.

ACCEPTING YOURSELF AS YOU ARE

There are things about ourselves that are easy to feel good about – perhaps for you it's your intelligence, your sporting skills or your singing voice... but it could be anything. When you think about these things, or when someone else pays you a compliment, it usually makes you feel proud and happy.

But everyone also has things about themselves that they find difficult to accept or feel good about. There might be things you feel shy or embarrassed about – perhaps you wish they weren't true. Again, it could be anything, and when you think about these things it can make you feel sad, and when someone notices or comments on them – even if they're not trying to upset you – it can feel embarrassing or even hurtful.

Having high self-worth means accepting all of yourself, even the parts that are difficult for you. This takes time and there's no rush or pressure. Let's explore this idea on the next couple of pages.

WHAT'S EASY TO FEEL GOOD ABOUT... AND WHAT'S HARD?

On or around the person below, write a few things that you find easy to love about yourself. These are the things you feel proud of, you want to share with your friends and family, and that you enjoy people noticing. There are no wrong answers, but if you need inspiration you could start with: my sense of humour, my guitar playing...

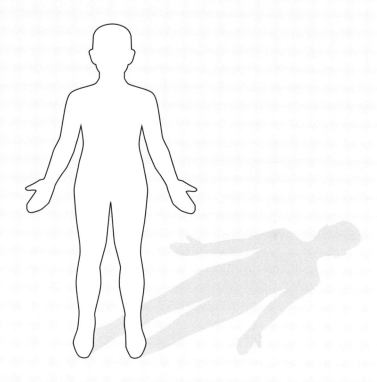

Now, in the person's shadow, can you write one or two things that you find harder to love about yourself? It can be something you want to hide or change – you can write whatever comes to mind.

It might have been tough to write those things down, or no big deal. However it felt, you're doing an amazing job.

HOW'S YOUR SELF-WORTH?

Now you've learned a bit about self-worth, how would you rate yours on a scale of one to ten? It's OK to go with your gut feeling – you're the expert on you.

1   2   3   4   5   6   7   8   9   10

**very low
self-worth**

**very high
self-worth**

Taking time to notice how you feel about yourself is helpful because:

★ **It helps you understand your emotions**

★ **It helps you understand your actions**

★ **It helps you work out when you might need extra support**

If you notice your self-worth is low, use this knowledge to take extra care of yourself. Turn to Part 5 to learn more about self-care.

I'M NOT GOOD AT EVERYTHING. I JUST DO MY BEST AT EVERYTHING.

Michael B. Jordan

PART 2:

WHAT INFLUENCES YOUR SELF-WORTH?

IT'S NOT YOU!

You have the power to strengthen and build up your sense of self-worth, but the biggest influences on your sense of self-worth are actually outside of your control. Becoming aware of how different things can boost or drain your self-worth is the first step toward building a strong foundation and unshakeable belief in yourself.

The more you understand yourself and the world around you, the easier it becomes to *be* yourself, whatever happens.

WHERE DOES SELF-WORTH COME FROM?

Your sense of self-worth and how easy it is for you to be your true self come from a complicated mix of things. Your experiences growing up, the media, school, your friends, as well as cultural influences all play a part in how you feel about yourself.

If you're a member of a minority group, society's attitudes toward your identity also play a part in how you see yourself. Plus, when you're a teen there's a bunch of new challenges: puberty, exams, navigating relationships, social media... these things can all affect your self-worth too.

With all this to contend with, it's really understandable if you struggle with self-worth, and find it hard to be your true self. But it's never too late to grow your self-worth and be happy in yourself.

Building up a strong sense of self-worth means your knowledge of who you are comes from within. Whether you fit in, what other people think and your experiences might knock your self-worth, but with a healthy sense of who you are you'll be resilient enough to get back to feeling good about yourself quickly.

SHOWING YOURSELF COMPASSION

Compassion is a sort of kindness. When you show someone compassion, you make the effort to understand them and treat their feelings with respect. You can show yourself compassion in the same way. When you feel sad, angry, worried or ashamed – perhaps because you've made a mistake or someone's hurt your feelings – showing compassion and curiosity toward your emotions will help them pass and help you understand yourself better.

Next time you're having a hard time, whatever the cause of it, you can show yourself loads of compassion. Saying an affirmation is a simple way of doing this. An affirmation is a positive, comforting message to yourself – saying them regularly helps rewire your brain for higher self-worth.

Try saying one or more of these affirmations to yourself:

It's understandable that I feel this way

I can take my time

This is really hard

I'll get through this

It's OK to take a break

What does my body need right now?

I don't have to be perfect

I can learn from mistakes

Other people's feelings and actions are outside of my control

I won't feel this way forever

When you're able to show yourself compassion during difficult or uncomfortable times, you create a safe place inside yourself where it's easy to be fully you.

MOOD DIARY

Does your mood go up and down sometimes? Maybe some days you feel confident, and on others you're more nervous and unsure of yourself. Changing moods are a normal part of life, and your self-worth can go up and down with your mood too.

Try keeping a mood diary for a week, to better understand yourself and how you respond to experiences. For each day, jot down the main things that happened in your life, then follow the prompts to explore how you felt.

MONDAY

What happened today?

Today I felt...
Today was good because...
Today was hard because...

Self-worth score

    1   2   3   4   5   6   7   8   9   10

TUESDAY

What happened today?

Today I felt...
Today was good because...
Today was hard because...

Self-worth score

    1   2   3   4   5   6   7   8   9   10

WEDNESDAY

What happened today?

Today I felt…
Today was good because…
Today was hard because…

Self-worth score

1   2   3   4   5   6   7   8   9   10

THURSDAY

What happened today?

Today I felt…
Today was good because…
Today was hard because…

Self-worth score

1   2   3   4   5   6   7   8   9   10

FRIDAY

What happened today?

Today I felt…
Today was good because…
Today was hard because…

Self-worth score

1   2   3   4   5   6   7   8   9   10

SATURDAY

What happened today?

Today I felt...
Today was good because...
Today was hard because...

Self-worth score

1   2   3   4   5   6   7   8   9   10

SUNDAY

What happened today?

Today I felt...
Today was good because...
Today was hard because...

Self-worth score

1   2   3   4   5   6   7   8   9   10

Taking time each day to pay attention to how you're feeling and record your self-worth levels helps you gain perspective on how your mood can go up and down from day to day. It's enough just to notice that however you feel is OK.

DITCH THE COMPARISONS

Comparing yourself to others – whether they're friends, celebrities or strangers on the internet – is always a drain on your self-worth. Even if you look down on someone and get a temporary boost of confidence from thinking you're better than them, relying on judging others in order to feel good about yourself will give you a shaky sense of who you are – plus it'll make you feel pretty lonely.

The truth is, you only ever see the highlight reel from other people's lives... especially online, but also in real life – you only really get to see or hear about the parts of people's lives and personalities they choose to show you. While you're seeing everyone's highlight reel, you're seeing and experiencing every moment of your own life – the behind-the-scenes as well as the highlights. It's no surprise that when you compare yourself to others, you usually end up feeling not good enough.

So, what's the answer? Comparing ourselves to others is really normal and we all do it. The trick is to remind yourself about the highlight reel. You'll never know anyone's full story – how hard they've had to work or all the mistakes they've made along the way. So next time you find yourself feeling down while scrolling through an influencer's perfect life, remind yourself:

These are only the parts this person is choosing to show me, this is not their whole story.

The same is true of anyone, even your best friend! You are unique and so is your life, so there's no need to put pressure on yourself to be more like anyone else.

THE POWER OF "YET"

Respecting and accepting yourself just as you are doesn't mean you can't also change and grow. We're all constantly learning and adapting, so naturally our personalities, opinions and thought patterns change over time.

A "growth mindset" is a brilliant way of allowing yourself to change while keeping your sense of self-worth high. A growth mindset shows respect for where you are right now, as well as all the potential you have inside you.

The opposite of a growth mindset is called a "fixed mindset". A fixed mindset can be both a sign and a cause of low self-worth; it's the idea that you're stuck where you are and aren't capable of change or progress.

So how do you cultivate a growth mindset? It can be as easy as adding one simple word: "yet". Try adding the word "yet" to the end of these sentences and see them transform from negative to positive:

I can't get the hang of algebra
Yet

I don't feel like I can be myself around my friends

I don't know how to do this

This problem doesn't make sense to me

I don't know all my lines in the play

Can you see how adding the word "yet" opens up the possibility of succeeding, just a little further down the line? Of course, just adding "yet" doesn't work for every situation, but by focusing on the journey toward your goals rather than where you are right now, you'll begin seeing your potential instead of just your challenges.

DISTORTED THINKING

As well as a fixed mindset, there are loads of different thought patterns that drag down self-worth and stop you from being yourself. The way we think has an incredible power and influence over how we feel, act and perceive the world.

How you think is as unique as your fingerprint, but there are a number of common thought patterns that are a drain on mental health and will make you feel terrible about yourself. Here are the main ones, and how to spot them:

All-or-nothing thinking: if this isn't perfect, I've failed completely

Over-generalizing: if one thing goes wrong, everything will go wrong

Focusing on the negative: if one thing goes wrong despite other things going right, that's the only thing I can think about

Fortune-telling: I know I'll fail

Mind reading: I know everyone will think badly of me

Catastrophizing: one mistake will ruin everything

Magnified thinking: the things I dislike about myself are the most important things about me; the things I like about myself aren't important

Negative comparison: my friend is better than me in every way

Unrealistic expectations: I should be perfect at everything

Putting yourself down: I'm a failure

Blaming yourself: everything goes wrong and it's all my fault

Feelings are facts: I feel ugly, so I must *be* ugly

Blaming others: if only people were nicer to me, I would be a better person

Do you recognize any of these thought patterns? Draw a circle around any that you find yourself thinking. Can you see how thinking in this way can bring down your sense of self-worth?

YOUR SELF-WORTH INFLUENCES

We've talked a lot about all the different things that can affect your self-worth, and of course these won't all affect you equally. The way your self-worth works is as unique as your fingerprint.

Here's a recap of the main things that influence young people's self-worth:

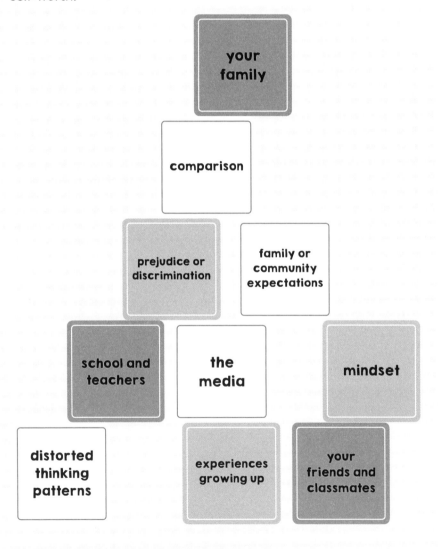

Have a think about the biggest drain on your self-worth. This will be something that gets you down, makes you feel like you're not good enough and like you need to hide your true self. What is it and how does it affect you? You can write more than one influence if that feels right:

Now write about what gives your self-worth a boost. This will be something that makes you feel calm, safe and able to be yourself. It might be a particular person, place or activity — it could even be a YouTube channel or a character from a book. Again, it's OK to write more than one here if it's hard to choose:

Recognizing who or what has a big effect on your sense of self-worth means you can show yourself extra compassion when you feel most vulnerable to low self-worth.

HOW CAN YOU GO FROM LOW TO HIGH SELF-WORTH?

Learning how to be yourself and build up your self-worth can feel really strange at times. If you've only just started thinking about self-worth, the way you think and feel about yourself probably just feels like the truth, and it's likely you assume everyone else thinks about you in the same way.

Beginning to challenge unhelpful thought patterns and be true to yourself can feel uncomfortable at first, but everyone has the power to raise their self-worth, and it's worth the effort. We're all different, so where you start from and how your mind works is unique to you. Working toward a healthy sense of self-worth involves carefully and patiently considering your own thoughts and actions, and slowly but surely shifting the way you see yourself.

Of course, there are ways to give yourself a boost (like getting a pep talk from a friend or acing a test), as well as things that will bring your self-worth down temporarily (like being dumped or told off), but we generally come back to around the same level of self-worth once we've moved on from these boosts and blips.

By taking the time to build up your inner sense of self-worth – the type that's based on a knowledge of who you are and what you deserve – you'll be able to come back to feeling good about yourself, whatever life throws at you.

WE CAN DO HARD THINGS.

Glennon Doyle

PART 3:
SELF-WORTH BOOSTERS

GIVE YOURSELF A BOOST

Everyone needs a boost of positivity sometimes. When you're feeling down, having a few quick fixes you can rely on to raise your self-worth in a hurry can be a lifesaver. Although they're temporary, boosts like these are a really important way of building self-worth, because they help get you out of your comfort zone and break cycles of negative thinking.

Read on for quick and clever ways to supercharge your self-worth.

MAKE A "BE YOURSELF" SHELF

Find a spot and dedicate it to things that make you feel good. Keeping feel-good things all in one place means you'll know exactly where to go when you're feeling down and need a boost.

Can you think of a shelf, drawer or corner of your room that could be just for you? If not, a box or rucksack works just as well.

What you put on your Be Yourself shelf (or box, or bag, or drawer...) is totally up to you. Fill it with good memories, reminders of your achievements, movies that make you laugh and books that make you smile.

Here are some ideas:

A shell from a day at the beach

Some amazing feedback from your teacher

Some amazing feedback from your teacher

Self-care reminders

A journal for writing in

Your favourite movie

A book of feel-good quotes

A soft, warm blanket

A letter to yourself (see pages 85–86)

Positive affirmations (see pages 53–54)

Great smelling moisturizer

What will you put on yours?
Jot down some ideas here:

POSITIVE SELF-TALK

Self-talk is the way we speak to and about ourselves – out loud or in our heads. Everybody does it, and having positive self-talk usually goes hand in hand with having high self-worth. If you have positive self-talk, you talk to and about yourself with kindness, generosity and understanding. If you have negative self-talk, it's the opposite – when you talk to yourself you're impatient and harsh, and you put yourself down when you talk about yourself with other people. Like most things, self-talk can change with your emotions.

What's your self-talk like?

Chances are, you're a little harsh on yourself. We could all do with showing ourselves more kindness, and this exercise will help you tap into more positive self-talk.

On the right are some examples of negative self-talk. Imagine you are someone very wise and kind – how would you respond to these, if someone said them about themselves?

Here's an example to get you started:

I always fail, what's the point in trying?

It's OK to be imperfect – you can learn from your mistakes.

All my friends secretly hate me

Why can't I just be like everybody else?

**I wish I wasn't so sensitive,
it's so embarrassing**

How did it feel to be that wise, kind character? If you can be wise and kind for this activity, you can speak to yourself in that way too. Practise next time you find yourself thinking negatively about yourself. Write down your positive self-talk or simply think it. It might feel awkward at first, but with time your positive self-talk voice will grow louder and more comfortable.

NOT TODAY, NEGATIVE SELF-TALK

Now you've tuned in to a more positive self-talk voice, you can see that you can have more than one voice inside you. The trick is to learn how to turn the volume up on the positive voices and down on the negative ones.

You can mute negative self-talk, just like an annoying online troll. Concentrate on the smaller, more positive voice inside you, and it'll slowly get louder. If you can't hear it yet, don't worry... you can find it in a positive affirmation (see pages 53–54), a favourite quote, imagining what your best friend would say, or even in this book.

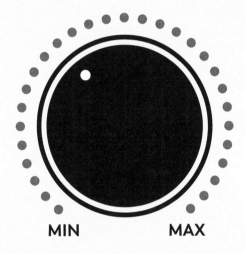

MIN   **MAX**

Next time you need a boost, close your eyes and imagine yourself turning the volume down on negativity, and up on positivity.

AFFIRMATIONS FOR SELF-WORTH

An affirmation is a short, positive message that strengthens your self-worth. The more you see, hear and say an affirmation, the more you'll believe it. That's because your mind takes time to absorb new ideas and get comfortable with them. Affirmations are a brilliant way to remind yourself just how amazing you already are.

Here's a bunch of affirmations for self-worth. Some of them will feel more effective than others, and that's fine – it's best to pick a maximum of two or three your mind can get really familiar with.

I am enough

I am worthy

I am fine just as I am

I am patient

I can take a break

I am strong

I can do hard things

I am a pleasure to be around

I am loved

I am already enough

I can do amazing things

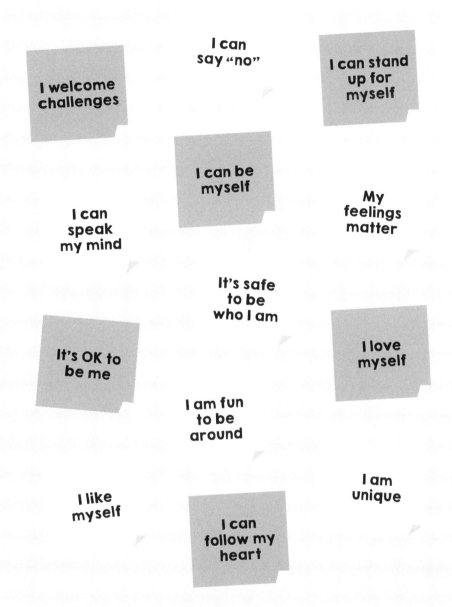

I welcome challenges

I can say "no"

I can stand up for myself

I can be myself

My feelings matter

I can speak my mind

It's safe to be who I am

It's OK to be me

I love myself

I am fun to be around

I like myself

I am unique

I can follow my heart

Once you've chosen two or three that appeal to you the most (or made up your own!), write them on a sticky note or piece of paper and stick them up somewhere you can see every day. The more you see, think about and say the affirmations, the better they will work.

SELF CARE IS HOW YOU TAKE YOUR POWER BACK.

Lalah Delia

DIY AFFIRMATIONS

Affirmations like the ones on the previous page are brilliant for raising self-worth and giving you the confidence to be your true self. Now it's time to create your very own, unique affirmation.

When an affirmation is really specific, the message your brain gets is even stronger. So you can say "I am confident" and feel that bit more confident... but if you say "I can walk into school with confidence", you can clearly picture yourself in that situation, acting with confidence.

Can you come up with an affirmation that's unique and specific to you? Perhaps there's a situation or activity that makes you feel like you're not good enough, or like you need to hide your true self. How could you send a positive message to your mind, using an affirmation?

To make an affirmation, you will need:

Positivity – **say what you are or will do, not what you aren't or won't do**

Yourself – **affirmations are about *you*, not anybody else**

Specificity – **be specific, keep your affirmation short and memorable**

The present tense – **talk as if the affirmation is already true**

Now it's your turn. Jot some ideas down, brainstorm and revise until you come up with an affirmation that's just for you. It's OK to cross out, make mistakes and play around with your ideas.

When you're ready, write your affirmation here:

PRIORITIZE HAPPINESS

What makes you feel happy? Perhaps it's something simple like a sunny day, or more complicated like the feeling of doing well at a sporting event. It could even be something you've enjoyed doing since you were little... it still makes you happy, but you might feel a bit embarrassed about it.

What makes you happy is as unique as you are, and making time for happiness is a powerful way of building self-worth.

So how can you prioritize happiness? Prioritizing something means putting it above other things, so you might put off doing your homework to enjoy a sunny evening in the garden with your family.

Putting happiness first doesn't mean ditching all the things that aren't your favourite... it's about placing importance on your enjoyment of life, and finding a good balance between what you want to do and what you *have* to do.

Jot down a few things – big or small – that make you feel happy:

examples: doodling, playing with my brothers, swimming in the sea

Quite often, even though there are things we love doing, we run out of time to do them because of the things we have to do – like homework – or the things we're in the habit of doing – like scrolling our phones. The key is to plan happiness into your day, and be flexible enough to take an opportunity for happiness when it comes along.

How could you plan happiness this week?

Put the things you have to do into this weekly planner, then see where you could move them around to make space for happiness, or add more things from your happiness list into your free time.

Monday	Tuesday	Wednesday	Thursday

Friday	Saturday	Sunday

Having a little (or a lot of) happiness every day will give you a regular boost, however you're feeling.

MINDFUL COLOURING

Studies have found that colouring is beneficial to emotional and mental health. It lowers stress and allows the mind to relax by focusing on one simple activity.

Relax and enjoy colouring this page.

CIRCUIT BREAKERS

Oh no! You're falling into a spiral of negative thoughts and your self-worth is taking a nosedive. It's time for an emergency circuit breaker to take control of your thoughts and get your emotions back into some kind of equilibrium.

These techniques focus on your body rather than your mind to help you feel more like yourself in no time.:

★ **Adjust your posture: sit or stand up straight, relax your shoulders and jaw.**

★ **Place your hand on your heart: concentrate on the feeling of your heart beating.**

★ **Breathe deeply: imagine your breath filling your lungs with oxygen, then emptying every last molecule.**

★ **Think about your feet: pull your focus away from your thoughts by concentrating on your feet.**

★ **Go outdoors: put your bare feet on grass or earth to ground your energy.**

★ **Shake it off: move your body vigorously to get rid of nervous energy and release tension.**

MAKE A TO-DAY LIST

Setting goals is really useful for keeping on track, staying true to yourself and improving motivation. But sometimes, setting goals that are too big or out of reach can have the opposite effect on your self-worth.

Making a to-day list is a quick and effective way of giving yourself an injection of confidence and feeling good about yourself again.

The difference between a to-do list and to-day list is that a to-day list includes everything – even the things you do without having to remind yourself. For example, you probably wouldn't put "clean my teeth" on a to-do list because it's part of your routine, but on a to-day list, it's all about recognizing your achievements, even the tiny ones.

Have a go at making a to-day list for today. You can include all the things you've already done – big and small – and tick them off as you write them. Think about the things you'd like to do with the rest of your day, as well as the things you need to do.

MY TO-DAY LIST

★ _____

★ _____

★ _____

★ _____

Ideas for your to-day list: daydream, write to a friend, eat a cookie, drink water, do one piece of homework

MY ACHIEVEMENTS

When you're feeling down about yourself it can be easy to forget how far you've come and all the things you've achieved along the way.

Achievements aren't just the type of things you get trophies or certificates for – although these are important too. Achievements can come in lots of different forms – from resolving an argument with a friend to learning to cook a meal for your family – and it's time to celebrate yours.

Can you think of something you've achieved for each of these trophies, medals and certificates? Write them on the plaques – if you feel like it, you can colour or decorate the pictures too.

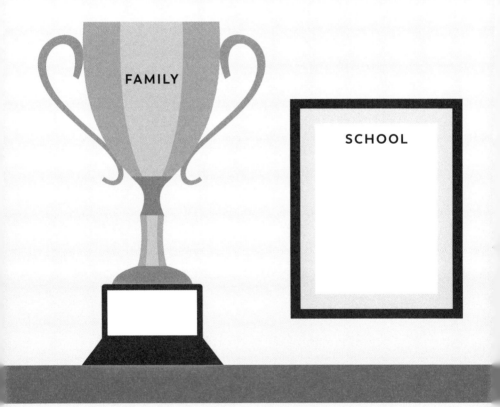

FRIENDSHIP

INDIVIDUALITY

JUST FOR ME

RANDOM

10 SELF-WORTH HACKS

1. Listen to your favourite music — **when you don't feel like yourself, a great song or playlist can remind you how much fun life can be.**

2. Journal — **writing your thoughts and feelings in a notebook or journal helps you make sense of them and get to know yourself a little better.**

3. Read a book — **fiction or non-fiction, a book will help you get out of your own head and escape into another world.**

4. Eat something delicious — **to enjoy the simple things in life.**

5. Take a shower — **getting clean will make you feel a fraction better.**

6. Get dressed up — **even if you have nowhere to go, putting on your favourite outfit will make you feel like your best self.**

7. Make your bed — **if your bed is a beautiful, orderly place to be, you'll automatically feel calmer when you're in it.**

8. Be kind — **showing kindness to others activates the parts of our brains responsible for self-worth and happiness.**

9. Let go of things that aren't "you" any more — **it's OK to leave things in the past if you no longer get enjoyment or value from them.**

10. Talk about your feelings — **choose someone you know and trust, and share your feelings with them.**

PART 4:

SHIFTING HOW YOU SEE YOURSELF

ARE YOU READY TO MAKE A CHANGE?

So far, we've learned loads about self-worth, and how difficult it can be to be yourself sometimes. Now it's time to start making real changes to how you think about and treat yourself – are you ready?

YOU ARE YOUR HARSHEST CRITIC

When your self-worth is low, it can feel like everyone is looking at you and judging you. You might feel hyper-aware of the parts of yourself you find hard to accept – like an aspect of how you look – and assume that everyone around you is also focusing on this.

The truth is, you are the one who thinks about yourself the most. Other people are thinking about themselves and their own insecurities. Unless you're a mind reader, there's no way of telling what other people are thinking about at any given moment... this can be frustrating but it's also freeing – you can choose what you believe other people are thinking. Are they thinking positive things about you... or not thinking about you at all? It doesn't really matter if it's accurate or not, because this exercise is just for you.

In doing this, you'll see that you can also choose your own thoughts. When a thought naturally comes up in your mind, imagine your brain is offering you a snack. Is it a snack you actually want to eat, or does it look a bit gross? If you don't want to eat the thought-snack your brain has offered you, simply choose another, tastier thought.

Which thoughts will you say "yes please" to? Write some positive, tasty thoughts on the snacks you'd like to eat.

I like myself

I can do this

my best is good enough

not good enough

everyone's laughing at me

there's something wrong with me

You can put unhelpful, negative thoughts here

THE FIVE PER CENT TRICK

Building a strong sense of self-worth can only be done one step at a time. It involves getting in the habit of being kind to yourself in big and small ways. When you make small changes and stick to them, soon they'll turn into big, positive changes to the way you think and feel about yourself.

An effective way of doing this is by regularly asking yourself how you could feel five per cent better. It's often as simple as having a glass of water, stretching your body, or talking to a friend. Even when you're feeling pretty good, you could probably feel even better, and when you're feeling down it's a great way to bring yourself some comfort and feel a bit more in control.

How could you feel five per cent better right now? Check out the ideas below, or come up with your own.

Grab an extra cushion

Drink some water

Go outside

Take a deep breath

Have a snack or meal

Take a nap

Text your best friend

Talk about your feelings

Write in a journal

Do some stretches

Do one thing on your to-do or to-day list

Tidy one part of your room

Change into comfier clothes

Put down your phone

Log off social media

Once you've come up with a way to feel five per cent better, do it! Check in with yourself and do the five per cent trick as often as you like.

SITTING WITH YOUR FEELINGS

We often hide our true selves because it feels too uncomfortable to do otherwise. The risk of feeling embarrassed or rejected or misunderstood is just too scary, so we stay small and try to fit in. Sometimes, it's a good idea to do what feels comfortable and safe – it would be exhausting and stressful to constantly throw ourselves out of our comfort zones.

But at other times, when it really matters, it's worth finding the courage to stand up and show who you really are inside. Like when someone's treated you badly, or is trying to get you to agree to something you don't want to do, it can feel incredibly difficult to stand up for yourself. That's when learning to sit with uncomfortable feelings is most useful.

Sitting with uncomfortable feelings means recognizing feelings of anger, anxiety, fear or sadness and not trying to fix or change them. It sounds simple but it's hard! Lots of the things we do – including scrolling on social media, lashing out at others and hiding our true feelings – we do in order to avoid feeling these uncomfortable feelings. Learning to sit with them is a skill. Here's how to do it:

Take a deep breath

Name what you are feeling
– silently or out loud

Be curious about
the feeling – where
is it in your body?
What thoughts
are coming up?

Notice the urge to
distract yourself
– on your phone,
lashing out or
by being busy
in some way

Remind yourself
that you are
safe and
show yourself
compassion

Keep breathing until the
feeling starts to pass

It takes time to master this, so be patient with yourself. Once you
learn how to do this, you'll be able to find the courage to do anything
and be your full self, whatever's happening.

FOCUS ON WHAT YOU CAN CONTROL

A lot of anxiety and low self-worth comes from the belief that we are in some way to blame for things other people do. The truth is, other people's thoughts, emotions and actions are completely outside of our control. Sure, we can have an influence on the people we meet and talk to, but ultimately we aren't able to control how other people see us, or what effect we have on them. With this in mind, it's clear that being yourself is the only way forward.

Reminding yourself of what you can and can't control, then focusing your attention only on the former is an effective strategy for calming racing thoughts and building self-worth.

Can you make a diagram that's personal to you? Perhaps there's someone who tries to blame you for their mistakes, or something you often worry about that's completely out of your hands.

What things are within and outside your control that you'd like to remind yourself of? For example, if someone called Emily tells you she thinks you aren't intelligent, that's her choosing to be cruel, not you or your intelligence causing her to make a comment. You could write "Emily's words" or "Emily's cruelty".

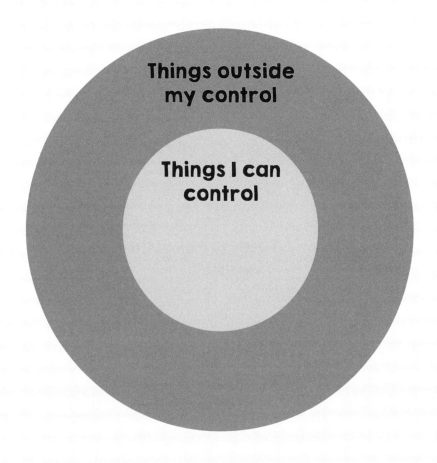

CHOOSE YOURSELF

Some people see putting yourself first as a selfish thing to do. It's often viewed as kind to give more importance to the feelings of other people than to your own. It's time to start thinking differently!

In fact, when you do what's right for someone else even when it's wrong for you, it leads to resentment and misunderstanding. It also denies the other person the opportunity to get to know the real you. The idea of upsetting someone else can be so overwhelming that you end up upsetting yourself instead.

Say you're doing an English project for school with a friend and you're deciding which book to research. Your friend wants to make a presentation about *The Great Gatsby* but you're much more inspired by *Frankenstein*. You could go along with your friend's ideas, keep quiet and study a book you're not that into. Or, you could speak up and make the case for *Frankenstein*. Speaking up for your ideas is choosing yourself. Even if you end up agreeing on *The Great Gatsby*, you've shown your interests and ideas to your friend, stood up for yourself and know each other a little better than before.

You have just as much right to speak your mind as anybody else.

SAYING "NO" AND SAYING "YES"

"Yes" and "no" can be two of the most difficult words to say. Saying "yes" to the things we really want can be intimidating and fill us with self-doubt. Saying "no" to the things we don't want can make us worry about upsetting other people.

Think about the things in life that you'd love to say "yes" and "no" to. Do you have a dream you want to fulfill, but the thought of trying feels terrifying? What would it be like to say "yes" to that dream?

I want to say "yes" to...

Is there something in your life that gets you down, that you dread and resent every second of? Imagine saying "no" to it.

I want to say "no" to...

Even though there are some things we just have to do (like studying) and things that aren't yet possible for you (like driving or moving out of your parents' house), getting to know exactly how you feel and what you'd say "yes" and "no" to in an ideal situation is an important part of growing your self-worth and being the real you.

TALK IT OUT

Talking about mental health can be difficult, to say the least. If you're struggling with low self-worth, talking about your thoughts and feelings with another person is going to be extra hard. When you don't feel good about yourself, your mind might trick you into thinking that nobody cares how you feel, or wants to help you.

While it's sadly true that not everyone knows how to react well to a conversation about emotions, there are people in your life who care and want to help. It's best to choose someone you already know and trust who is kind and respectful – that might be a parent, carer, teacher, friend or relative.

Talking about your feelings is brave and powerful. When we talk about what's troubling us with someone who's a good listener, those difficult emotions get easier to handle.

It can be hard to know what to say, so use these tips to help you start the conversation:

★ **Remember you don't need to come up with a perfect explanation for how you feel; just do your best.**

★ **You also don't need to come up with solutions – just sharing is enough.**

★ **To make it less intense, talk while you're doing something else – like walking the dog, in the car or making dinner.**

★ **If you feel awkward or worried about the conversation, say so!**

★ **If you have an idea of what might help you, suggest it – the other person may be able to help.**

★ **Don't wait for the perfect time – today is a good day to make a change.**

WHO CAN I TALK TO?

Write down the person (or people) you feel comfortable talking to about your feelings. What makes them good to talk to?

If you can't think of anyone you trust enough to talk to, you can always turn to your school counsellor or doctor for confidential advice. There are also resources on page 139 – you're not alone and help is available.

WHEN WE SPEAK

WE ARE AFRAID OUR WORDS

WILL NOT BE HEARD

NOR WELCOMED.

BUT WHEN WE ARE SILENT,

WE ARE STILL AFRAID.

SO IT IS BETTER TO SPEAK.

Audre Lorde

COPING WITH CHANGE

Perhaps it's starting to feel a bit easier to be yourself day to day, or maybe it still feels quite difficult. Either way, the most challenging times for your sense of self-worth are during periods of change.

So many changes happen when you're a teen: school, friendships, relationships, puberty, the way you think, what you want out of life... the list goes on. Change can mess with your head, so it's no surprise that when a change happens – whether it's big or small, unexpected or planned for – your sense of who you are can feel a bit shaky.

When change happens, it's time to use all the skills you have to strengthen your self-worth and stay true to yourself.

practice self-care	focus on what you can control
look for positives	turn down the volume on negative self-talk
take care of your body and mind	be compassionate towards your feelings

THROW AWAY NEGATIVITY

Some unhelpful, distorted or negative thoughts and habits are hard to let go of. Is there something you do, or a way of thinking that you recognize is hurting your self-worth, but you can't seem to shake it?

Letting go of these things takes time, so be really patient with yourself. There's no quick fix, but psychologists believe that finding a way to physically throw these thoughts or habits away helps to release them from your mind too.

Try this chalk and pebble trick to throw away the things that bring you down.

You will need:

Rocks or pebbles

Chalk

What to do:

Use the chalk to write the thing or things you'd like to throw away on the rocks or pebbles.

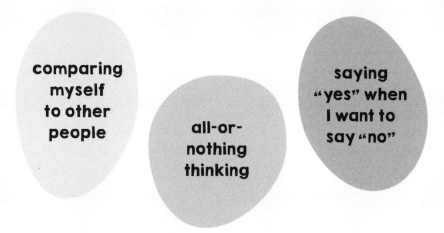

Now take your pebbles somewhere it's safe to throw them (like a lake, or river or seashore), and throw them into the water. As you throw, imagine the things you want to throw away flying out of your body.

PRACTICE MAKES PROGRESS

Have you ever heard of perfectionism? It's the idea that everything you do should be perfect, flawless and that you should make zero mistakes, ever. Perfectionism is also a big sign of low self-worth. This is because perfectionism is all about having zero compassion for yourself when you make a mistake, need help or even come second place instead of first. It's about believing who you are is never quite good enough.

Sound familiar? If this is you, don't worry – it's possible to break free from perfectionism. Trying and failing is part of being human – it's not something any of us can avoid. The answer lies in learning to feel OK being a beginner and understanding that everything in life takes practice. Walking, talking, making friends... even texting took you time to master, and finding new things to practise doesn't stop as you get older.

Like watching a plant grow from a seed, you get a little closer to your goal each time you practise. Try celebrating the small wins and steps in the right direction.

DEAR PAST AND FUTURE ME...

Who you are changes over time, and that's OK. It's useful to think about how you've changed, and what you hope for in the future. Being kind, curious and patient through changes is a sign of high self-worth, and a great thing to cultivate in yourself.

Think back two years: what's changed about you, and what's pretty much the same? What might you have wanted to know from your future self back then? Try writing your past self a letter:

Dear past me...

If you had a time machine and could visit yourself two years in the future, what would you want to know? What hopes and worries do you have? Write a letter here:

Dear future me...

KEEP A GRATITUDE JOURNAL

Looking for positive things is a brilliant way to learn to appreciate your life and focus on the ways in which you're lucky and grateful to be you. Writing in a gratitude journal is a simple way to get in the habit of finding, recording and remembering small, good things every day. Try making gratitude journaling a part of your night-time routine for one week and see how you get on. You can write in this book, or use it as a template for your journal or notebook.

Monday
I'm grateful for...

1. _____

2. _____

3. _____

Tuesday
I'm grateful for...

1. _____

2. _____

3. _____

Wednesday
I'm grateful for...

1. _____

2. _____

3. _____

Thursday
I'm grateful for...

1. _____

2. _____

3. _____

Friday
I'm grateful for...

1. _____

2. _____

3. _____

Saturday
I'm grateful for...

1. _____

2. _____

3. _____

Sunday
I'm grateful for...

1. _____

2. _____

3. _____

If you enjoyed gratitude journaling, you can carry on doing it for as long as you like. All you need is a pen or pencil and something to write on. If you miss a day, don't worry, you can just pick it up again when you're ready.

I TRY TO START EVERY DAY AND END EVERY DAY BY TAKING A MOMENT TO BE GRATEFUL.

Olivia Wilde

PART 5:

TAKING CARE OF YOURSELF

YOU ARE IMPORTANT

As you grow more independent, taking care of yourself will become more and more down to you. Self-care isn't just about the basics – like showering and eating healthily – it's about your whole self: physical, mental and emotional.

Low self-worth can make self-care difficult sometimes. If you're more concerned with what other people think than with your own needs and feelings, it's hard to put yourself first when you need to. You might even feel like there's not much point in things like getting enough sleep, eating healthy food and exercising.

A healthy sense of self-worth means taking care of yourself even when it's hard. The more care and attention you show yourself, the more confident you'll feel being your full self.

WHAT IS SELF-CARE?

You might have heard the phrase "self-care" being used, but what exactly does it mean?

Self-care means taking care of your needs so you can be your best, healthiest self. Your needs can be anything from staying hydrated to taking time away from a friend who's treating you badly. Self-care is anything that improves your well-being by taking care of yourself.

I like to wind down by drawing in my sketchbook.

I read a chapter of a book before going to sleep at night.

I bring a bottle of water with me wherever I go.

When someone acts aggressive or disrespectful toward me, I walk away.

I do one piece of homework each day, so I don't have to do it all at once.

I like to sleep late at the weekends.

As you can see, self-care can be all sorts of things. How do you care for yourself?

CARING FOR YOUR BODY

Your body is changing in loads of different ways. Some of them you can see – like hair growth and getting taller – and some you can't – like hormone changes and brain development. Your teenage body is incredibly resilient, but it also needs lots of care and attention to help you through all these changes. Follow these simple tips to stay healthy:

Keep water handy:
sip water throughout the day to keep your body and brain functioning well

Eat plenty of fruit, vegetables, iron and protein:
these are the food groups that keep your body strong, healthy and energized

Move your body:
gentle exercise will keep your body healthy and your emotions regulated

Wash daily:
shower, brush your teeth and hair to stay fresh and clean as your body grows

Sleep well:
teens need around 9 ½ hours of sleep every night

Wear sunscreen:
protect your skin from sun damage

SLEEP TRACKER

How do you feel after a bad night's sleep? Chances are, you feel pretty bad. When you don't get enough sleep, your body doesn't get a chance to recharge its batteries, so you feel like you're running on empty the next day.

This can also affect your sense of self-worth and confidence. When you're well-rested, you're better able to believe in yourself and make wise choices.

Getting enough shut-eye can be a challenge sometimes. Early school start times and a natural change to your sleeping habits during puberty – teenagers' body clocks mean you're more prone to stay up late and struggle to get up early in the morning – make it a bit of a balancing act. Try keeping a sleep tracker for a week by adding approximate times to the tracker.

Aim for 9 ½ hours' sleep per night

Tips for tired days:

Drink loads of water
Take things one step at a time
Be kind to yourself
Take a nap if you can
Put off anything that can wait until tomorrow

	Fell asleep	Woke up	Total hours sleep
Monday			
Tuesday			
Wednesday			
Thursday			
Friday			
Saturday			
Sunday			

Bedtime routine

Having a routine will help you fall asleep quicker and more easily. Aim for:

Soft lighting
No screens
Do things in the same order each night

POSITIVE BODY IMAGE ISN'T BELIEVING YOUR BODY LOOKS GOOD, IT'S KNOWING YOUR BODY IS GOOD, REGARDLESS OF HOW IT LOOKS.

Lindsay and Lexie Kite

WALK IT OFF

Exercise doesn't need to be a chore. If you're into competitive sport, enjoy sport at school or are part of a club already, that's brilliant. If you're not so sporty, learning how to take care of your body through exercise can be more difficult, especially if you have feelings of low self-worth in relation to how your body looks.

Moving your body helps keep it healthy, but it also helps your mental and emotional well-being too. This is because movement helps calm your nervous system, reduces stress and anxiety, and raises happiness levels. Studies have shown that simple exercise like walking helps raise self-esteem and boosts your mood.

Here are some tips to help get you walking:

★ **Wear comfortable shoes**

★ **Bring plenty of water**

★ **Wear sunscreen**

★ **Bring a friend to chat to**

★ **Walk to somewhere you enjoy being**

★ **Make a playlist of positive music**

★ **Plan your route**

★ **Stay safe and tell someone where you're going**

Draw a map of your walking route. Perhaps you already have a favourite place to walk – you can draw it here. If not, you can use the space to plan a route:

SOCIAL MEDIA AND YOU

Studies carried out by Facebook have found that social media has a negative effect on young people's mental health. Because of the focus on appearance, social media can give the impression that who you are is not as important as how you look. Even if you know that this isn't true, looking at social media for a long time every day will train your brain to place more importance on appearance and fitting in, than on being yourself.

32 per cent of teen girls feel worse about their bodies after using Instagram

While social media can also be a place to find like-minded people, discover new artists and connect with friends, you can get the most out of it by using it consciously and having boundaries around your screen time.

TIPS FOR CUTTING DOWN SCREEN TIME AND SOCIAL MEDIA

Take it slow – if you spend lots of time online, your brain won't be used to being bored. Take breaks from screens and gradually make them longer.

Apps can help you – download an app to manage your screen time and lock you out of certain apps and websites between set times.

Write down your feelings – it might be tough, so have a journal handy for writing down your emotions.

Try a dumb phone – these are mobile phones that have calls and texts, but no internet or apps.

Ask for help – sit down with your parent or carer to come up with a screen time schedule.

Handle with care – be mindful of your emotions when you're online. If something's upset or angered you, it's OK to unfollow or block – you don't need to give it any of your energy.

Be kind – be mindful of the fact that everyone you come across online is a human being with feelings and self-worth, just like you.

If you're worried about how you use the internet or something that happened online, you can always talk to a trusted adult about it. There are also resources on page 139.

HOW TO UNWIND

What do you do to relax?

Relaxing doesn't need to be expensive or photo-friendly. Just looking out of the window, doodling or tidying your room can be really relaxing.

Here's a relaxing activity that will help your mind and body unwind. Try it when you're feeling frustrated, anxious or annoyed – all you need is a pen or pencil. Don't worry about getting the lines perfect – the trick is to relax and let your doodles flow.

Fill this box with little circles:

Fill this box with lines:

Fill this box with zigzags:

Doodling helps lower stress, lift your mood and unlock creativity.

MEETING YOUR EMOTIONAL NEEDS

Emotional needs are the things you need in order to feel safe, loved and OK just as you are. A lot of the time, you'll be able to care for your emotions yourself, but we all need to connect with others sometimes too.

All human beings need to feel:

* **Safe**

* **Loved**

* **Understood**

* **Accepted**

If we don't feel those things, it's incredibly challenging to feel safe enough to be ourselves. Just like we all need food, water and sleep, we also need to feel calm and safe around the people we spend most of our time with. These people have a big effect on your emotions, and the way you feel about yourself most of the time helps shape who you are.

There are lots of ways we look to others to help meet our emotional needs – asking for a hug or a chat, using social media, asking for reassurance or advice, or doing activities with others. It's always OK to ask for attention, love and reassurance from those around you.

What makes you feel safe, loved, understood and accepted is different for everybody. What's the best way for someone to show you that they care. Draw a circle around your top five, and add your own if you like:

Compliments

Giving a small gift

Giving a thoughtful gift

Praising something you've worked hard on

Spending time together

Helping with homework

Giving hugs

Giving a high-five

A thoughtful text

Going on a trip together

A funny text

Chatting together

Running errands together

Working together on a project

Listening

Saying "I love you"

Saying "I'm proud of you"

Cooking your favourite meal

Driving you places you need to go

Helping you work out a problem

Knowing what's important to you

Paying attention to you

Asks about your day

Cuddles you

Sticks up for you

Eating meals together

Gives you space when you ask for it

Respects your privacy

Hanging out together

ALMOST EVERYTHING

WILL WORK AGAIN

IF YOU UNPLUG IT

FOR A FEW MINUTES,

INCLUDING YOU.

Anne Lamott

PART 6:

I'LL BE ME AND YOU BE YOU

RESPECTING OTHERS AND RESPECTING YOURSELF

Being yourself is quite simple when it's just you. But when you throw other people into the mix, things get more complicated and challenging. Learning how to be yourself and hold on to your sense of self-worth in any situation is a skill that will set you up for life. In this chapter, we'll look at all the different ways there are to be yourself, and how to keep your self-worth high, whoever you're with.

ROOM FOR EVERYONE

There are seven billion (and counting) ways of being yourself – as many as there are human beings on the planet. It's a cliché, but it's true: the one thing we all have in common is that we're all unique.

When you have low self-worth, it can feel like there isn't space for you to be yourself, because it might upset or inconvenience someone else trying to be *them*selves. The truth is, there is enough space for you to be yourself, and for everybody else too. We'll certainly emotionally affect each other sometimes, but the trick is to remember that other people's appearance, choices and actions are both out of your control and not about you.

For example, when your friend gets a new pair of trainers and wants to show them off to you, it probably isn't to compare them to your trainers and make you feel bad, it's to show you the trainers they're excited about. Other people's actions tell you all about them, and not much about you (it's your own actions and reactions that tell you about yourself).

Even if someone is criticizing you, it's still about them. Perhaps someone says something unkind about your body size: this tells you about what they value, how much respect they have for you and crucially, how they feel about their *own* body.

Confused? Here's how it works:

We all have our insecurities — the things we find hard to love and accept about ourselves. These take up a lot of headspace and we typically put a lot of importance on them, thinking about them loads more than the things we're happy with.

This affects how we see the world. For example, if you find it hard to accept how your body looks, you'll be more likely to notice other people's bodies, and judge them like you judge your own.

In short, we see the world how we see ourselves. The more we understand this about ourselves and each other, the easier it becomes to be yourself, and feel comfortable with others being themselves.

WHAT IS RESILIENCE?

Resilience is the ability to bounce back and feel OK again when difficult things happen. Resilience does *not* mean ignoring your feelings, pushing through when you need a break or pretending you're fine when you're actually struggling.

Say you fail an important test at school – that's bound to hurt. There's the fact you might have to take the test again, but also all the emotions that come from failing. Perhaps in that situation you'd tough it out and act like you don't care. Or maybe you'd feel so embarrassed that you quit the subject all together. A resilient response to this would be somewhere in the middle: take some time to feel your feelings, then when you're ready you can make a new plan.

The key to resilience is flexibility. When things don't go your way, resilience means you can easily respond to changes by revising your expectations and plans, while being mindful and gentle with your emotions.

This random doodle game is all about seeing potential and finding a creative way forward. All you need is a pen or pencil.

Take a look at each random shape – can you make them into drawings? You can make them into animals, objects, faces, landscapes... see where your imagination takes you!

You can play the random doodle game with a friend – draw a shape each then swap and make the other's shape into a drawing. It's cool to see what you each come up with, and being creative together is a brilliant way to build a strong friendship.

A NOTE ON RESPONSIBILITY

Another big part of resilience is the ability to take responsibility for your actions and the part you play in your life, without blaming yourself for things you can't control or getting overwhelmed by feelings of shame. Sometimes, you'll do things you regret – the resilient way to deal with these times is to allow yourself to feel your emotions, then take some time to repair. Repairing might mean apologizing, or rethinking your approach to a particular task. Everyone messes up sometimes – the mark of a resilient person with high self-worth is that they take time to put it right.

BE CONSCIOUS ONLINE

Being conscious means staying aware of your own emotions. This is extra hard when you're on social media, as there's so much other stuff going on to distract you from your own feelings. Because of this, it can be hard to notice when social media is having a negative effect on your emotions and self-worth.

Next time you're using social media or interacting with others online, take a moment to check in with your emotions using these questions:

What emotion/s am I feeling?

Are my shoulders and jaw tense or relaxed?

How's my breathing?

How's my sense of self-worth?

1   2   3   4   5   6   7   8   9   10

How am I benefitting from this website/app?

If you notice that you feel calm and good about yourself, that's great. If you realize that you're feeling tense and bad about yourself, take a break. It's OK to use the internet in ways that benefit you, but leave out the parts that drain your energy and self-worth.

FRIENDSHIPS AND SELF-WORTH

The people you spend time with have a big effect on your sense of self-worth. The way you feel about yourself when you're around your friends, whether you can be yourself and how you treat each other influences how you feel about yourself, and this will ripple out into other areas of your life.

These questions will help you reflect on your friendships:

Who is in your circle of friends?

Can you think of one word to describe each friend?

If you had a problem you were embarrassed to talk about, would you feel able to turn to your friends?

In what ways are you similar to your friends?

In what ways are you different?

If you disagreed with a friend about something, would you feel able to tell them?

Being mindful of how good your friendships feel helps build up your self-worth. When you're aware of how other people make you feel, you can make informed choices about how close you want your friendships with them to be.

WHAT MAKES A GOOD RELATIONSHIP... AND A BAD ONE?

If you struggle with low self-worth, it's quite common to find yourself in friendships or relationships with people who make you feel like you can't be yourself around them. This isn't your fault. People with low self-worth tend to blame themselves for any problems or conflicts, making it hard to spot when someone's not a good fit for them.

Arm yourself with knowledge about the signs of a good and bad friendship or relationship, so you can feel confident in standing up for yourself against bad treatment.

Positive signs	Negative signs
Likes you when you're being yourself	Puts you down and wants you to change
Is OK with you having other friends	Tries to control who you see
Replies to your messages	Ignores or ghosts you
Is considerate of your feelings	Acts as if your feelings don't matter
Is interested in your opinions	Wants you to agree with them on everything
You feel safe around them	You feel anxious or unsafe around them
Is respectful to you, even if they're angry	Is a completely different person when they're angry
If they've upset you, you can tell them	Will not accept responsibility for their actions

If you start to stand up for yourself, you may find negative friendships naturally change and become less close, or even end. This can be painful, but it's far, far better to hang out with yourself or a smaller group of friends than with someone who treats you badly.

WHAT TO DO IF YOU'RE IN A BAD FRIENDSHIP OR RELATIONSHIP

If you're in a friendship, relationship or any kind of situation with another person where you feel unsafe or like you can't leave, it's not your fault. This can happen to anyone and the blame lies with the person treating you in a controlling or disrespectful way.

They may try to make you feel guilty or scared to stop you from leaving, so remember: you get to choose which friendships and relationships you're a part of.

There are many people you can talk to if you're in this situation, or unsure about someone in your life. A friend or adult that you know and trust will want to listen and help you. You can also check out page 139 for more resources. You're not alone and you deserve good, healthy friendships and relationships.

LIFE IS TOO SHORT
TO WASTE YOUR TIME
ON PEOPLE WHO
DON'T RESPECT,
APPRECIATE
AND VALUE YOU.

Roy T. Bennett

BEING YOURSELF IN AN IMPERFECT WORLD

Emotionally, we usually feel safest and most comfortable when we feel like we fit in with the people around us. This is just how the human brain and nervous system have evolved: getting to know people who are different to us in some way feels like a risk to our safety-conscious brains.

The more secure we feel about our own sense of self, the more comfortable we are with difference of any kind. Feeling anxious or threatened by difference is often a sign of low self-worth, and it's OK if you feel this sometimes. What's not OK is when it comes out as disrespect toward yourself or others.

For lots of reasons, many people feel anxious about the differences between us – and these feelings of anxiety often do come out as some form of disrespect. For most of history, people who are different to those in power have been oppressed, controlled and exploited, so it's no wonder that, as society moves forward and begins to confront this history (and how exploitation, discrimination and violence still happen today), that it brings up a lot of feelings... these are uncomfortable subjects.

But just because they're uncomfortable, that doesn't mean they shouldn't be talked about. Showing respect to ourselves and each other and being conscious of our own emotions is the way we all become more understanding, more ourselves and more gentle with the world around us. You alone cannot fix the world's problems, but you can make a positive difference. Be yourself, do your best and you will contribute toward making the world a place in which more and more people can be themselves fully and safely.

GET TOGETHER TO MAKE A DIFFERENCE

Linking up with friends is a great way to build confidence and have your voice heard. You don't have to agree on everything – in fact, it's really important to have a free, open and critical mind in order to respect other people – but when you're united over something that's important to you, it's a powerful thing.

Ways to work together include:

Start a petition

Organize an after-school club

Write to your government representatives

Have a meeting with your teachers

Create group artwork with a message

Raise money for a charity

Is there a cause or subject you feel strongly about? Sketch ideas for a poster or online graphic here to spread your message.

Make sure it has:

An eye-catching image

A memorable slogan

A positive and respectful message

A call to action (like a website to visit or a meet-up to attend – these don't need to be real yet, just play around with ideas!)

DON'T SPEND ALL OF YOUR TIME TRYING TO BE LIKE SOMEONE ELSE BECAUSE YOU CAN NEVER BE THEM AND THEY CAN NEVER BE YOU.

Raven-Symoné

PART 7:

SELF-ACCEPTANCE

BEING OK WITH WHO YOU ARE

In this book there's a lot about standing up for yourself and knowing exactly who you are and what you want. That's important, but it's also important to understand that you won't always feel totally certain about these things – and that's OK too. True self-worth means knowing that you are, and will always be, a work in progress, accepting yourself at every stage and learning to enjoy the process of becoming more and more yourself.

WHAT IS ACCEPTANCE?

Acceptance is about living in the moment. It's about seeing reality, rather than a perfect or catastrophic version of it – seeing things as they are, not how you'd like them to be. Accepting reality doesn't mean you're OK with it, or think it's fair... and it doesn't mean you can't work or ask for help to change the things you think need changing. It simply means acknowledging where you are.

Acceptance sounds like this:

> My family isn't going abroad for a holiday this year.

> I got a detention for late homework.

> My best friend isn't talking to me.

Self-acceptance means owning and welcoming all of yourself, even the parts that make you feel embarrassed or anxious, or like you don't belong. When you practise self-acceptance, you become your own best ally, able to ask for support when you need it and letting go of the need to put pressure on yourself.

Self-acceptance sounds like this:

> I'm struggling to get to sleep at the moment, because I feel anxious.

> I'm pleased with the mark I got in my exam.

> I get nervous around boys/girls my age.

I ACCEPT MYSELF

Now it's your turn to practise acceptance. Think about how things are for you right now, and write three things that you accept as they are. Remember – acceptance doesn't mean that you support these things. They can be positive (like a trip you're excited about) or negative (like an annoying sibling you have to share a room with) parts of life.

I accept...

SHOWING KINDNESS TO EVERY PART OF YOURSELF

We all have things about ourselves that we'd like to change. Perhaps you can't wait to grow taller, or you wish you were more confident, or you wish your straight hair was curly (or your curly hair was straight!) – it's part of being human to want to change things about yourself.

A strong sense of self-worth involves accepting these things about ourselves, even when we wish they were different.

Here's a way of showing kindness to those things you'd like to change:

Think of something about yourself that you'd like to change. Close your eyes and imagine you are holding it gently in your hands like a small, cute animal. Speak to it softly (out loud or in your head) – you could say «I've got you» or «you're safe here» or even «I love you». When you're ready, imagine placing it somewhere warm and comfortable to sleep.

Imagining your characteristics in this way helps you show compassion to yourself, and focusing on the parts that you find most difficult to accept is an effective way of building self-acceptance.

CHECK IN WITH YOURSELF

Taking a little time to check in with yourself before responding – whether it's to a post on social media, a text from a friend or a big decision – will help you get to know yourself better and make choices you really believe in.

Even if you're 99 per cent sure of the right thing to do, it's worth pausing to investigate that one per cent, identify what you're really feeling and consider what might be clouding your judgement.

If you have trouble with self-worth, this is probably going to be a challenge. It's always OK to take your time to reply to texts or other notifications – you don't owe anyone an immediate response (unless it's an emergency). Practise these phrases to help give yourself time to check in with yourself:

I need a little time to think about that

Let me call you back

I'm not ignoring you, just considering my answer

I'm confused – can I ask some questions?

You're also able to simply not respond in many situations. If you see something online, you're always free to scroll past it without responding; and if someone's speaking or texting you in a way that makes you feel scared or insulted, you can simply ignore or walk away from them.

A body scan is a great way to check in with yourself. You'll notice emotions and tension that can otherwise go undetected. Plus it's really relaxing.

Here's how to do it:

Sit or lie comfortably; somewhere quiet where you won't be disturbed.

Think about the top of your head, then let your awareness travel very slowly down your body.

Notice any feelings, sensations or discomfort in your body.

Notice anywhere you feel tense or heavy.

Notice any thoughts that are coming up, and let them float gently away.

Keep moving down your body until you get to the tips of your toes.

Try a body scan any time you need to get clear about how you're feeling.

PERMISSION TO CHANGE

You are great just as you are, *and* it's OK to change and grow. It might sound like a contradiction, but the two things can both be true.

All human beings change – getting older, having new experiences and encountering new ideas will change how you think, feel and behave in big and small ways. You don't have to stay the same for anyone, and it's OK to change your mind about things that were once what you wanted. You're always evolving into a new version of yourself, and you have the power to accept yourself at every stage of your evolution.

Are there any ways you can feel yourself changing at the moment? Perhaps you feel your self-worth growing, or you're developing a new skill.

MAKE A SELF-ACCEPTANCE POSTER

Add your favourite affirmation in the centre of the poster below – use cool lettering and colour to make it really stand out. When you're finished, cut it out and stick it somewhere you'll see it every day.

I LIKE WHAT I DO,
AND I LIKE HOW I DO IT.
I LIKE MY MISTAKES
AND I LIKE THE PACE AT WHICH
I LEARN FROM MY MISTAKES.
I DON'T WANT TO BE
ANYBODY ELSE BUT ME.

Zoe Saldana

SHIFT YOUR WORDS

Low self-worth can trick you into thinking you're either too much or not enough. Sometimes, you may fall short or give too much of yourself – like if you fail a test or put a lot of energy into a friendship that doesn't work out – but when these things happen, they don't mean that *you* are too much or not enough.

The ability to separate who you are inside from the things you do and happen to you is sometimes hard. Adjusting the way you speak about yourself helps – try these simple switches.

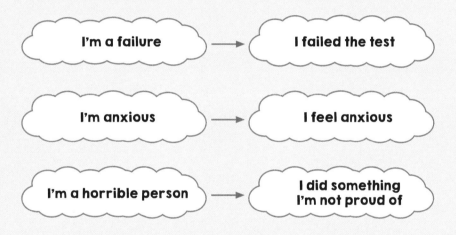

Can you see how a small change in language shifts the sentences from being about who you are as a person, to being about a specific, temporary situation? Research shows that using language in this way helps you grow self-acceptance and emotionally process difficult experiences more quickly.

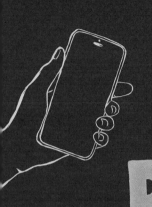

PART 8:

LOOKING FORWARD

JUST BE YOU

As simple and as complicated as it is, being yourself is something you can work on every day. From the smallest decisions – like which flavour doughnut you'll have – to the big life choices – like which subjects to study – as long as you follow your own inner compass, you will always be growing to be more and more yourself.

Some days, being yourself will feel easy – enjoy these, you deserve it. Other days won't be so easy. You'll make choices where choosing yourself means upsetting someone else or missing out on an opportunity, or you'll make mistakes and other people will try to bring you down. These tough days happen when you're living life to its fullest – they don't mean you're doing anything wrong.

Being yourself is a lifelong project, and now is a brilliant time to start.

RULES TO LIVE BY

Say what you mean

Stand up for yourself and others

Use your voice

Walk away from disrespect

Speak kindly to and about yourself

Choose yourself

You are just fine, exactly as you are

PLAN OF ACTION

How will you take what you've learned in this book and use it in your life? Jot down notes or make a plan here:

Near the beginning of the book, you rated your self-worth out of ten. How's your self-worth right now?

1 2 3 4 5 6 7 8 9 10

**very low
self-worth**

**very high
self-worth**

Perhaps it's gone up thanks to what you've learned in this book, or perhaps it's lower or about the same. Lots of things affect self-worth, and growing it is a process, so it's OK to be where you are. You're doing great.

YOU'RE NOT ALONE

I used to be friends with a group of girls who all dressed exactly the same. I didn't feel good in those clothes but I was worried they wouldn't be friends with me if I dressed how I wanted. Eventually I got sick of it and started wearing outfits I actually felt good in. Surprisingly, my friends complimented me and slowly – without anyone really saying anything – they all started dressing a bit more individual too. I guess they were inspired by me.

Nadia, 14

I was staying up late every night just scrolling on my phone, which was making me tired in the day as well as affecting how I felt about my body because of the type of apps I was on. It wasn't until my phone screen smashed and I had to go a couple of days without it that I realized how addicted to it I was, and how rubbish it made me feel about myself. Instead of another smartphone, I got one of those cheap brick phones that just does texts and calls. My friends sometimes tease me but I actually feel loads better.

Cooper, 16

I got a text from a friend saying a girl in our class had been disrespectful to him and we all had to block her on our phones and not talk to her at school. It didn't feel right so I ignored the text and carried on as normal at school. I ended up sticking up for the girl; people were treating her really badly. It turned out to have been the boy who was in the wrong – I'm not really friends with him any more.

Elena, 11

I've known I was gay since I was quite young, but decided not to tell anybody until I was a bit older – when I would start uni perhaps. That felt far enough in the future to take the pressure off myself. But then last year my cousin came out as a lesbian. She's quite a bit older than me and said she'd been wanting to tell the family for years but had been too scared. Seeing her do that gave me the courage to tell my parents about my sexuality. It feels great to be my true self around them.

Archie, 13

ASKING FOR HELP

If you're struggling with low self-worth, or any other aspect of your mental health, there are lots of organizations out there you can turn to for help and advice. If you feel like your sense of self-worth is starting to have a negative effect on your life, it's a good idea to talk to a trusted adult and make an appointment with your doctor.

Be Real Campaign
berealcampaign.co.uk
Campaign to change attitudes towards body image, encouraging people to put health above appearance and feel body confident.

BEAT
0808 801 0711
beateatingdisorders.org.uk
Helpline, web chat and online support groups for people with eating disorders, such as anorexia and bulimia.

Campaign Against Living Miserably (CALM)
0800 58 58 58
thecalmzone.net
Provides listening services, information and support for anyone who needs to talk, including a web chat.

Childline
0800 1111
childline.org.uk
Support for young people in the UK, including a free 24-hour helpline.

FRANK
0300 123 6600
talktofrank.com
Confidential advice and information about drugs, their effects and the law.

The Jed Foundation
1 800 273 8255
jedfoundation.org
Information and advice for US teens to promote emotional and mental health.

National Alliance on Mental Illness (NAMI)
1 800 950 6264
nami.org
Information and advice on managing mental health for US teens.

On My Mind
annafreud.org/on-my-mind
Information for young people to make informed choices about their mental health and well-being.

Refuge
0808 2000 247
refuge.org.uk
Advice and support for domestic abuse.

Stem 4
stem4.org.uk
Advice, information and apps for teen mental health.

Young Minds
youngminds.org.uk
Information about every aspect of mental well-being for young people.

FURTHER READING

Check out these books for teens about self-worth, mental health and being yourself:

Be True to Yourself
Amanda Ford

The Girl Guide: 50 Ways to Learn to Love Your Changing Body
Marawa Ibrahim

Taking Up Space: The Black Girl's Manifesto for Change
Chelsea Kwakye and Ore Ogunbiyi

Positively Teenage
Nicola Morgan

You are a Champion: How to Be the Best You Can Be
Marcus Rashford and Carl Anka

Just as You Are
Michelle and Kelly Skeen

You are Awesome
Matthew Syed

A Girl's Guide to Being Awesome
Suzanne Virdee

Wolfpack (Young Reader's Edition)
Abby Wambach

The Self-Care Kit for Stressed-Out Teens
Frankie Young

CONCLUSION

You are a good, loveable person, even when you don't feel like it. Being yourself is harder than it seems, and sometimes we lose sight of what it really means. You exist for you, not for anybody else, and you don't need to live by anyone else's expectations.

You do not need to explain or label yourself, you don't need to fit in, and you only need to make sense to yourself. It takes a lot of courage to be in the world and follow your own path. You are a whole, complicated human being and it's a privilege for anybody to be your friend. It's OK to just be you!

YOU ARE PERFECTLY CAST IN YOUR LIFE. I CAN'T IMAGINE ANYONE BUT YOU IN THE ROLE. GO PLAY.

Lin-Manuel Miranda

Have you enjoyed this book?
If so, why not write a review on your favourite website?

If you're interested in finding out more about our books,
find us on Facebook at **Summersdale Publishers**, on Twitter at
@Summersdale and on Instagram at **@summersdalebooks**
and get in touch. We'd love to hear from you!

Thanks very much for buying this Summersdale book.

www.summersdale.com